The Benefits of Wudhu

(Ablution)

In Islam

For Body Health & Spiritual Healing

English Version

by

Jannah Firdaus Mediapro

2022

*Best Drought Tolerant Grass Plant for Hot Desert Climates Zone
Bilingual Edition*

Jannah Firdaus Mediapro

Publishing

2022

Best Drought Tolerant Grass Plant for Hot Desert Climates Zone
Bilingual Edition

Prolog

"O you who have believed, when you rise to [perform] prayer, wash your faces and your forearms to the elbows and wipe over your heads and wash your feet to the ankles." — (The Holy Quran Al-Ma'idah: 6)

Islam faith emphasizes the importance of purifying our bodies since it strengthens our souls, ultimately bringing us closer to the One who is the Creator of all.

Best Drought Tolerant Grass Plant for Hot Desert Climates Zone Bilingual Edition

Chapter 1 History of Wudhu

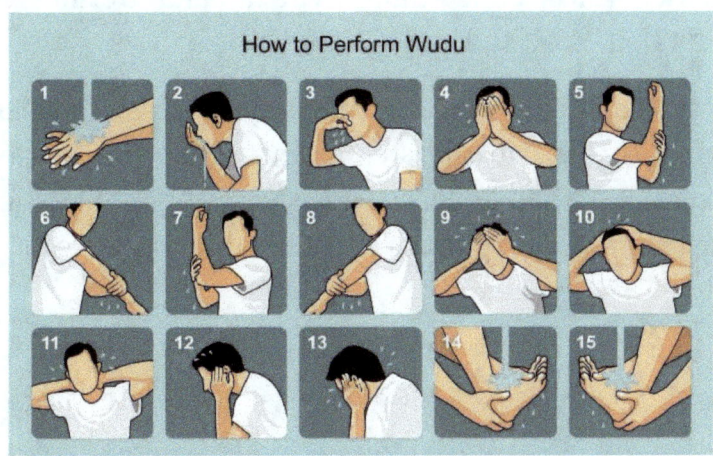

All Muslims perform ablution (Wudhu) before offering prayer or reciting the The Noble Qur'an. This is a simple yet obligatory practice of washing certain body parts, including one's hands, feet, arms, mouth, nostrils, ears, and face.

Not to mention, while performing Wudhu purifies our body, it also induces great health benefits that positively affect our mental and physical wellbeing.

Wuḍhu is the Islamic procedure for cleansing parts of the body, a type of ritual purification, or ablution.

The 4 Fardh (Mandatory) acts of Wudu consists of washing the face, arms, then wiping the head and the feet with water. Wudu is an important part of ritual purity in Islam.

It is governed by fiqh (Islamic jurisprudence), which specifies rules concerning hygiene and defines the rituals that constitute it.

It is typically performed before prayers (salah or salat). Activities that invalidate wudu include urination, defecation, flatulence, deep sleep, light bleeding, menstruation, postpartum and sexual intercourse.

Chapter 2

The Benefits of Wudhu For Body Health

Wudu is often translated as 'partial ablution', as opposed to ghusl as 'full ablution' where the whole body is washed. It also contrasts with tayammum ('dry ablution'),

which uses sand or dust in place of water, principally due to water scarcity or other harmful effects on the person. Purification of the body and clothes is called taharah.

Here are some tested and proven benefits of ablution that attest to the importance of it for us as Muslims:

1) The Act of Ablution Reduces Stress & Depression

Our religion claims wudhu or ablution as a therapeutic experience, especially for those suffering from depression.

In point of fact, several yoga experts encourage these days to perform Wudhu before going to bed, saying it relaxes our mind and bodies, ensuring a good night's sleep.

2) Keeps Our Skin Looking Fresh & Young

Performing Wudhu refreshes our skin by opening our skin pores, removing fatigue, and cleaning all the dust accumulated while dispersing sweat and fats.

3) Plays a Vital Role In Good Oral Hygiene

Ablution includes purification of the mouth such that it removes any food particle remains from our teeth, tongue, and gums, preventing oral health issues. It also strengthens our facial muscles and gets rid of bad mouth odors.

4) Keeps the Germs From Entering Our Bodies

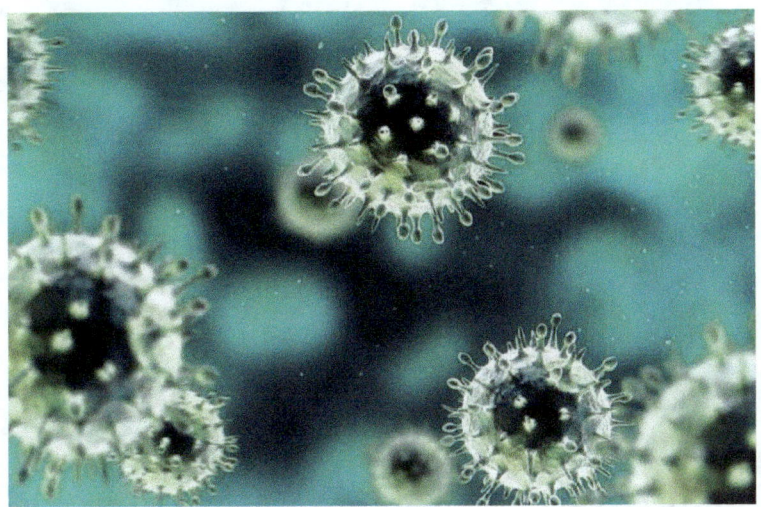

Not to mention, rinsing nostrils when performing Wudhu ensures no germs are getting trapped in our nose follicles, which effectively prevents the germs from entering our system.

5) Prevents Ear Wax Buildups

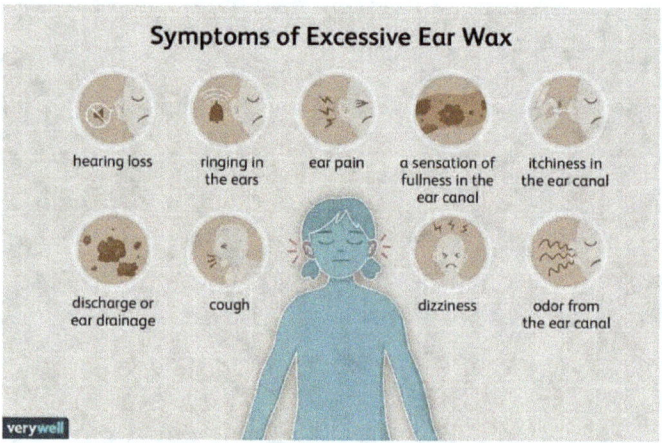

Furthermore, rinsing the insides and outsides of our ears during ablution removes the extra wax layer, preventing mastoiditis from arising while putting a stop to wax buildups.

6) Strips Our Skin Of Hidden Bacteria & Virus

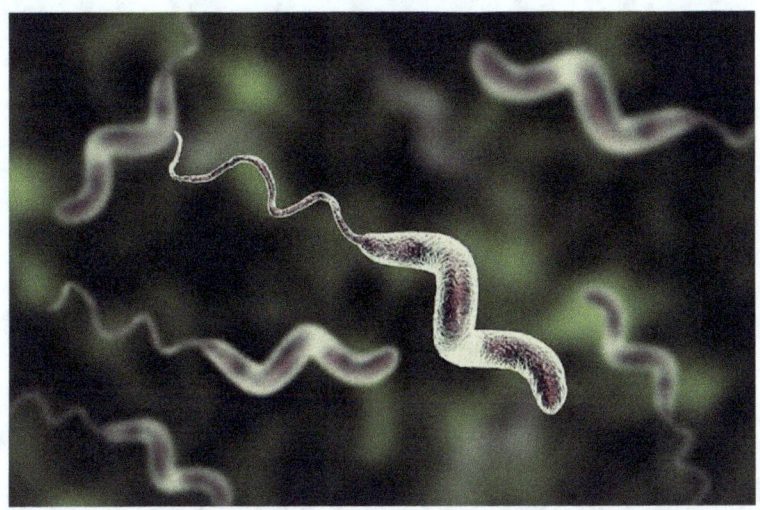

Washing between our toes and fingers removes those germs and bacteria that stay well-hidden otherwise.

7) Improves Blood Flow and Mental Health Healing

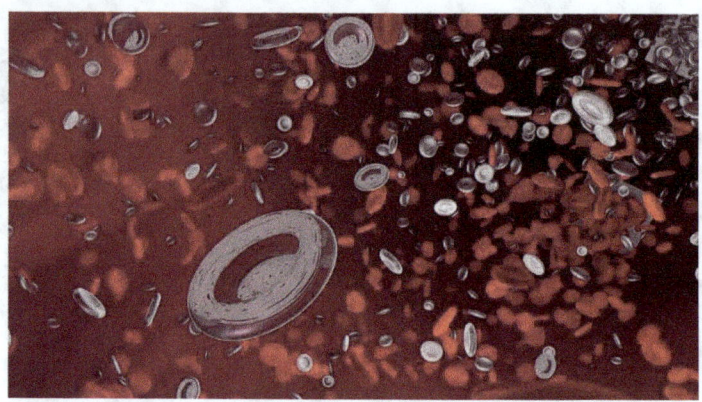

It is proven that putting pressure on certain points of our arms improves our overall blood flow, and performing ablution ticks all the right boxes in this aspect.

There are three major veins in our elbows connected to our brain, heart, and liver, and putting pressure on them gives our body strength both physically and mentally.

Chapter 3 The Blessing & Reward of Wudhu In Akhirah

The wudu of a believer is indicative of the position that cleanliness holds in Islam. Being the key to Salah, a mu'min will perform wudu at least 5 times a day. Therefore, utmost care should be taken in perfecting it.

By implementing the following sunnats and guidelines extracted from the noble Ahadith of Rasulullah (sallallahu 'alayhi wasallam), one would Insha Allah be able to achieve maximum reward for the wudu.

1) Expiation of sins

- "He who performs the *Wudu* perfectly (i.e., according to Sunnah), his sins will depart from his body, even from under his nails." [Muslim]

- He who performs *Wudu* like this, his previous sins will be forgiven and his Salat and walking to the mosque will be considered as supererogatory act of worship." [Muslim].

- "When a Muslim, or a believer, washes his face (in the course of *Wudu*), every sin which he committed with his eyes, will be washed away from his face with water, or with the last drop of water; when he washes his hands, every sin which is committed by his hands will be effaced from his hands with the water, or with the last drop of water; and when he washes his feet, every sin his feet committed will be washed away with the water, or with the last drop of water; until he finally emerges cleansed of all his sins." [Muslim]

2) The Prophet will recognize his Ummah from their traces of Wudu

- Abu Hurayrah reported: The Messenger of Allah (*sal Allahu alayhi wa sallam*) went to the (*Baqi`*) cemetery and said, "May you be secured from punishment, O dwellers of abode of the believers! We, if Allah wills, will follow you. I wish we see my brothers." The Companions said, "O Messenger of Allah! Are not we your brothers?" He said, "You are my Companions, but my brothers are those who have not come into the world yet." They said; "O Messenger of Allah! How will you recognize those of your Ummah who are not born yet?" He said, "Say, if a man has white-footed horses with white foreheads among horses which are pure black, will he not recognize his own horses?" They said; "Certainly, O Messenger of Allah!" He said, "They (my followers) will come with bright faces and white limbs because of *Wudu*; and I will arrive at the *Haud* (*Al-Kauthar*) ahead of them." [Muslim]

3) The Believers will be recognized by their traces of Wudu on the Day of Judgment

- "On the Day of Resurrection, my followers will be summoned '*Al-Ghurr Al-Muhajjalun*' from the traces of Wudu'." [Al-Bukhari and Muslim] This name is explained as:

- *"The word "Ghurr" is the plural of "Agharr" which means shining or white. It is used for animals (like a horse), i.e., a white mark on its face. Here, it refers to that radiance which will issue from the brows of the believers on the Day of Resurrection and which will make them prominent.* Muhajjalun *is from* Tahjil *which also means whiteness but it is used for that whiteness which is found on all the four or at least on three legs of a horse. Here, it refers to that light which will shine through the hands and feet of the believers because of their habit of performing Wudu. This means that the believers among the Muslims will be distinguished from other communities by virtue of the radiance issuing from their faces, hands and feet on the Day of Resurrection in the same way that a horse with a white forehead is easily distinguised from other horses."*

4) Wudu is a radiance and the Believers are encouraged to increase in it.

- Abu Hurayrah (*radi Allahu anhu*) said, "Whoever can increase the area of his radiance should do so." [Al-Bukhari and Muslim]

5) An Angel will seek forgiveness for you

- It is narrated from ibn Umar that the Messenger of Allah said, "Purify these bodies, and Allah will purify you.

- Whenever a slave sleeps in a state of purification, an angel sleeps within his hair and he does not turn over during the night except that he [the angel] says:

- O Allah, forgive Your slave, for he went to sleep purified." [at-Tabarani and graded "good" by Sh Al-Albani]

6) The adornment of a Believer in Jannah will reach up to where the water reached his body.

- "The adornment of the believer (in *Jannah*) will reach the places where the water of *Wudu* reaches (his body)." [Muslim]

7) Saying the supplication after wudu is a means of entering Jannah

- "Whoever of you performs *Wudu* carefully and then affirms: `Ash-hadu an la ilaha illallahu Wahdahu la sharika Lahu, wa ash-hadu anna Muhammadan `abduhu wa Rasuluhu* [I testify that there so no true god except Allah Alone, Who has no partners and that Muhammad is His slave and Messenger],' the eight gates of *Jannah* are opened for him. He may enter through whichever of these gates he desires (to enter)." [Muslim]

8) Preserving wudu is a sign of emaan

- "… and no one preservers their *wudu* except a Believer." [Ibn Maajah, Authentic according to Sh. Al-Albani]

9) Performing Wudu in hardship effaces the sins and elevates the ranks

- The Prophet (*sal Allahu alayhi wa sallam*) said, "Shall I not tell you something by which Allah effaces the sins and elevates ranks (in *Jannah*)?" The Companions said; "Certainly, O Messenger of Allah." He said, "Performing the *Wudu* thoroughly in spite of difficult circumstances, walking with more paces to the mosque, and waiting for the next *Salat* (the prayer) after observing *Salat*; and that is *Ar-Ribat*, and that is *Ar-Ribat*." [Muslim] The scholars say:

"Hardship and unpleasantness here stand for the uneasiness that one feels while performing Wudu *in severe cold. To wait for the next* Salat *after offering a* Salat *is regarded as* Ribat *for the reason that by so doing, a person who is particular in offering* Salat *keeps himself constantly engaged in the obedience and worship of Allah to keep Satan away from him."*

Chapter 4 Epilogue

Consequently, we can find multiple Prophet Muhammad SAW Al-Hadith and verses in The Noble Qur'an that emphasize the importance of purifying our bodies.

It is that part of our faith in Allah SWT (God) that gives us mental, spiritual, and physical health benefits, all in equal measure.

*Best Drought Tolerant Grass Plant for Hot Desert Climates Zone
Bilingual Edition*

Author Bio

"Indeed, those who have believed and done righteous deeds – their Lord will guide them because of their faith.

Beneath them rivers will flow in the Gardens of Pleasure.

Their call therein will be, 'Exalted are You, O Allah,' and their greeting therein will be, 'Peace.'

And the last of their call will be, 'Praise to Allah, Lord of the worlds!'"

(From The Holy Quran)

Best Drought Tolerant Grass Plant for Hot Desert Climates Zone
Bilingual Edition

www.ingramcontent.com/pod-product-compliance
Lightning Source LLC
LaVergne TN
LVHW052233110526
838202LV00095B/202